How to Raise
YORKSHIR

By
Arthur Liebers and Dana Miller

Distributed in the U.S.A. by T.F.H. Publications, Inc., 211 West Sylvania Avenue, P.O. Box 27, Neptune City, N.J. 07753; in England by T.F.H. (Gt. Britain) Ltd., 13 Nutley Lane, Reigate, Surrey; in Canada to the book store and library trade by Clarke, Irwin & Company, Clarwin House, 791 St. Clair Avenue West, Toronto 10, Ontario; in Canada to the pet trade by Rolf C. Hagen Ltd., 3225 Sartelon Street, Montreal 382, Quebec; in Southeast Asia by Y.W. Ong, 9 Lorong 36 Geylang, Singapore 14; in Australia and the south Pacific by Pet Imports Pty. Ltd., P.O. Box 149, Brookvale 2100, N.S.W., Australia. Published by T.F.H. Publications, Inc. Ltd., The British Crown Colony of Hong Kong

ACKNOWLEDGMENTS

Pictures were taken by Heyer of Three Lions, Inc., with the cooperation of Miss Sunny Shay and Grandeur Kennels, Hicksville, Long Island, N. Y.

ISBN 0-87666-410-9

© 1978 by T.F.H. Publications, Inc.

Contents

1. HISTORY OF THE BREED.. 5

2. SELECTING YOUR YORKSHIRE TERRIER PUPPY...................... 7
   A Healthy Puppy . . . Male or Female? . . . Adult or Pup? . . . The Puppy's Papers . . . The Pedigree

3. CARING FOR THE YORKSHIRE PUPPY.. 11
   Bringing Your Puppy Home . . . The Puppy's Bed . . . Feeding the Puppy . . . Watching the Puppy's Health . . . Worming . . . The Useful Thermometer . . . Some Canine Diseases . . . Coughs, Colds, Bronchitis, Pneumonia . . . Major Diseases of the Dog . . . The Female Puppy

4. HOUSEBREAKING AND TRAINING YOUR YORKSHIRE............ 23
   He's a Terrier . . . Paper Training . . . Puppy Discipline . . . Chewing . . . Barking . . . Climbing on Furniture . . . The Too-Friendly Puppy . . . Kids in the Family . . . Walking on Lead . . . Curb Training the Yorkie

5. BASIC OBEDIENCE TRAINING FOR THE YORKSHIRE............ 31
   Training to Sit . . . The "Lie Down" . . . The "Stay" . . . The "Come" on Command . . . Heeling . . . "Heel" Means Sit, Too . . . A Review . . . Advanced Training and Obedience Trials

6. GROOMING THE YORKSHIRE TERRIER...................................... 43
   The Coat . . . Other Care . . . The Coat Takes Time

7. SHOWING YOUR YORKSHIRE TERRIER.. 57
   How to Enter . . . Getting Your Yorkie Ready for a Show . . . Standards of the Breed

8. BREEDING THE YORKSHIRE TERRIER.. 62
   Size Is Important . . . Pre-Natal Care . . . Whelping . . . Weaning the Puppies

The tiny Yorkshire Terrier is intelligent and courageous—a delightful pet.

Bred originally to sniff out and catch rats for Welsh miners, today's Yorkie retains all of his inquisitiveness and gameness for creatures that move.

1. History of the Breed

Fanciers of the breed expect the Yorkshire Terrier to become, in time, even more popular than the Poodle with the American dog-owning and dog-loving public. The "Yorkie" is one of the most appealing of the toy dogs. In a 2- to 4-pound package, he combines a high degree of canine intelligence, courage surprising in such a small dog, inherent good manners and a delight-

ful pixie-like appearance. He is one of the hardiest of the toy breeds and resists disease well, despite his fragile appearance. As a household pet, the Yorkie has much to recommend him. He is loyal, has a sweet disposition and does not shed, which, from the point of view of the woman of the house, gives him a high rating.

Much of the desirability of the Yorkie stems from the fact that he has retained the characteristics of his ancestors. The Yorkshire today is basically the same dog that was used by the miners of the Yorkshire section of England as a "ratter" in the coal mines. By instinct he is a hunter with much heart. Although the ancestors of the present-day Yorkie were much larger dogs, weighing 10 to 14 pounds, today's toy-sized dog is reduced only in size, not in spirit or capability.

Unlike some other breeds which were developed by wealthy breeders, the Yorkshire Terrier was a workingman's dog. Because many breedings, unrecorded in any stud book, finally developed the true Yorkshire Terrier type, his exact origin is unknown. One theory has it that the Yorkie came from crosses between the Clyesdale and Black-and-Tan Terriers. It was only in the 1860's that the British Kennel Club recognized the Yorkshire as a true breed. Looking back in time almost a hundred years, it is possible to imagine the miners gathering at the local pubs on Saturday afternoons to compare their dogs and to determine which points to breed for, mating smaller specimens generation after generation until the Yorkie arrived at his present "toy" size.

The modern Yorkshire Terrier owes his appearance and character largely to a remarkable dog that died in 1875—Huddersfield Ben. During his showing career he was often winner in his class, topping all other Terriers. Fortunately he had the power of transmitting his virtues to his progeny, and he was a highly prolific stud dog. Since his time, the breed has been well established and puppies come true to color and type.

In all essentials Huddersfield Ben possessed the points required of a Yorkshire at a modern show. A judge might consider his tail a bit too long, and his muzzle a bit longer than the modern preference, but the popular Yorkie of today carries the genes of this dog in his body and will pass them on to future generations.

2. Selecting Your Yorkshire Terrier Puppy

At about eight weeks of age—when puppies are usually offered for sale—the young Yorkie gives no indication whatever of how he will look as a grown dog. In selecting your puppy you must depend, then, on the reliability of the breeder or seller. You might want to write to the Yorkshire Terrier Club of America—which has recently been recognized by the American Kennel Club as the official club sponsoring this breed—for a list of its members or breeders in your vicinity.

If you are planning to buy a puppy with show prospects you should be prepared to spend in the neighborhood of $150 for one whose lineage shows that he has good show possibilities. A Yorkie that you want solely as a pet should be considerably less expensive. And the smaller the dog, the higher the price, since size and coat are the two outstanding characteristics of the breed.

Yorkies are born completely black, with tiny markings of tan above the eyes, under the tail and on the legs. With their flat puppy coats, they look like miniature Welsh or Airedale Terriers. As they grow older, the coat gets heavier, color starts to break through and you can see the desirable steel-blue color making its appearance. If the color shows as early as four months, the puppy will probably grow into a light-colored dog which is not desirable in the show ring, but is preferred by many owners as being more attractive than the darker, standard color. (For the Standard, see page 59.) When the puppies are about five days old, the breeder will probably have their tails cropped ⅓ off, to the preferred length.

A HEALTHY PUPPY

The healthy puppy will be active, gay and alert, with bright, shiny eyes. He should not have running eyes or nose. He should have a sturdy, shortish

Regular grooming and care will give your Yorkie the long, silky, uncurled hair and the "falls" that are characteristic of the breed. Bringing a dog to championship condition takes a lot of effort—but it is worth it.

body with a straight back. While you may want a small dog, be wary of taking the "runt" of the litter as there may be some physical reason for his small size. In buying a puppy—especially a higher-priced one—it is always wise to make your purchase subject to the approval of a veterinarian. The seller will usually allow you eight hours in which to take the puppy to a vet to have his health checked. However, come to a clear agreement on what happens if the vet rejects the puppy. It should be understood whether rejection means that you get your money back or merely choice of another puppy from the same litter.

If you are unfamiliar with Yorkshire puppies you may think that they look moth-eaten, and they do, but that's normal. It takes about a full year for the dog to come into his adult coat.

MALE OR FEMALE?

With Yorkshires, it doesn't make much difference whether you obtain a male or a female unless, of course, you want to breed your pet and raise a litter of puppies. Both sexes are pretty much the same in disposition and character. In addition, possibly because of their small size, the Yorkie females often do not come into season twice a year as do most other breeds, so that you have less of a problem with "suitors" or with staining during the period of heat. However, if you are planning to breed your female puppy, try to get a larger specimen — one that will weigh about five pounds at maturity so that bearing puppies will be easier. It is often necessary to undergo the expense of a Caesarean birth when a smaller female is mated.

If you choose a female but decide you don't want to raise puppies, your dog can be spayed and will remain a healthy, lively pet.

ADULT OR PUP?

Whether to buy a grown dog or a small puppy is another question. It is undeniably fun to watch your dog grow all the way from a baby, sprawling

In the early days of its development as a breed, the Yorkie was a much larger dog. Now it is bred primarily as a companion and comforter though its independence and spunkiness has not been lost in translation.

and playful, to a mature, dignified dog. If you don't have the time to spend on the more frequent meals, housebreaking, and other training a puppy needs in order to become a dog you can be proud of, then choose an older, partly trained pup or a grown dog. If you want a show dog, remember that no one, not even an expert, can predict with 100% accuracy what a small puppy will be when he grows up.

If you have a small child it is best to get a puppy big enough to protect himself, one not less than four or five months old. Older children will enjoy playing with and helping to take care of a baby pup, but at less than four months a puppy wants to do little but eat and sleep, and he must be protected from teasing and overtiring. You cannot expect a very young child to understand that a puppy is a fragile living being; to the youngster he is a toy like a stuffed dog.

THE PUPPY'S PAPERS

If you are investing in a purebred dog, obtain the necessary papers from the seller, especially if you are planning to show or breed your dog. Usually the litter will have been registered with the American Kennel Club. This is necessary before the individual puppy can be registered. The breeder should provide you with an Application for Registration signed by the owner of the puppy's mother. Then you select a name for your dog (it must be 25 letters or less, and cannot duplicate the name of another dog of the breed, or be the name of a living person without his written permission). Enter the selected name on the form, fill in the blanks that make you the owner of record, and send it to the American Kennel Club.

THE PEDIGREE

The pedigree of your dog is a tracing of his family tree. Often the breeder will have the pedigree of the dog's dam and sire and may make out a copy for you. Or, you can write to the American Kennel Club once your dog has been registered and ask for a pedigree. The fee depends on how many generations back you want the pedigree traced. In addition to giving the immediate ancestors of your dog, the pedigree will show whether there are any champions or dogs that have won obedience degrees in his lineage. If you are planning selective breeding, the pedigree is also helpful to enable you to find other Yorkies that have the same general family background.

3. Caring for the Yorkshire Puppy

BRINGING YOUR PUPPY HOME

When you bring your puppy home, remember that he is used to the peace and relative calm of a life of sleeping, eating and playing with his brothers and sisters. The trip away from all this is an adventure in itself, and so is adapting to a new home. So let him take it easy for a while. Don't let the whole neighborhood pat and poke him at one time. Be particularly careful when children want to handle him, for they cannot understand the difference between the delicate living puppy and the toy dog they play with and maul. If the puppy is to grow up loving children and taking care of them, he must not get a bad first impression.

Yorkies are friendly, affectionate dogs that appreciate their human companions, but children must be taught to handle them carefully since their small size makes them more vulnerable to injuries than larger dogs.

If you have more than one Yorkie, first train them individually, then make walks a family affair.

THE PUPPY'S BED

It is up to you to decide where the puppy will sleep. He should have his own place, and not be allowed to climb all over the furniture. He should sleep out of drafts, but not right next to the heat, which would make him too sensitive to the cold when he goes outside. If your youngster wants to share his bed with the puppy, that is all right, too, but the puppy must learn the difference between his bed and other furniture.

You might partition off a section of a room — the kitchen is good because it's usually warm and he'll have some companionship there. Give him a pillow or old blanket for his bed, a bowl of water, and cover the floor with a thick layer of newspapers.

You have already decided where the puppy will sleep before you bring him home. Let him stay there, or in the corner he will soon learn is "his," most of the time, so that he will gain a sense of security from the familiar.

Give the puppy a little food when he arrives, but don't worry if he isn't hungry at first. He will soon develop an appetite when he grows accustomed to his surroundings. The first night the puppy may cry a bit from lonesomeness, but if he has an old blanket or rug to curl up in he will be cozy. In winter a hot water bottle will help replace the warmth of his littermates, or the ticking of a clock may provide company.

FEEDING THE PUPPY

By the time a puppy is eight weeks old, he should be fully weaned and eating from a dish. Always find out what the seller has been feeding the puppy as it is well to keep him on the same diet for a while. Any sudden change in a puppy's feeding habits may cause loose bowels or constipation.

Common sense is your best guide to feeding your Yorkshire puppy properly. Until he is about seven or eight months old, the puppy should be

The Yorkie's topknot is a trademark of the breed. When putting in the topknot, hair is parted on a line even with the corner of the eye and brushed upward.

fed three times a day; then cut him down to two feedings and after a year, he should manage nicely on one feeding a day.

Two heaping tablespoons of food is a meal for a Yorkie. However, if yours acts hungry, add a bit more to his dish; if he snubs a meal, just take it away and don't offer him any food until his next feeding time. As to what to feed the puppy, you have a wide choice. Fresh beef or meat is probably the best food, but don't get the more expensive leaner cuts of meat. The lower-priced hamburger grind at your butcher or the supermarket contains a lot of fat that your dog needs in his diet. If you buy canned dog food, study the label carefully and make certain that it contains a large proportion of meat. Many kennels feed their dogs exclusively on kibble — the broken-biscuit type of dog food or the meal that comes in bags or cardboard containers. If you feed the dried food, add some beef fat or bacon drippings occasionally. On almost all packages of food you'll find the feeding directions for puppies and adult dogs and you won't go wrong if you follow them. However, there is a big difference in the quality of canned dog foods — the higher-priced cans usually contain much more actual meat then the lower-priced.

In addition to the basic food, you should give your dog an occasional egg (scrambled or hard-boiled), cottage cheese, green vegetables or grated carrot, and cod-liver oil, wheat germ or vitamin supplement. If you find that your puppy or older dog persistently refuses a certain food, don't force him to eat it. He may know best.

The puppy's food should be served at room temperature, never hot or cold. And of course you won't let your dog near chicken bones or fish with bones that can catch in his throat or tear his intestines.

According to the latest research on dog nutrition, cow's milk is not a desirable dog food. It differs considerably from the mother dog's milk and many dogs are unable to get much benefit from it. In addition, many Yorkies develop loose bowels from cow's milk.

If you are using a food that has to be mixed with a liquid, use lukewarm water or any bland soup rather than milk. Keep in mind that your dog's digestive system is more like a wolf's than a human baby's. Your tiny dog needs the same foods that a German Shepherd or a Boxer needs, just less in quantity.

WATCHING THE PUPPY'S HEALTH

The first step in protecting the health of your puppy is a visit to the veterinarian. If the breeder has not given your puppy his first distemper shots, have your vet do it. You should also have your Yorkie protected against hepatitis, and, if required by local law or if your vet suggests it, against rabies. Your puppy should receive his full quota of protective inoculations, especially if you plan to show him later. Select a veterinarian you feel you can trust and keep his phone number handy. Any vet will be glad to give a regular "patient" advice over the phone — often without charge.

Yorkies and children are a wonderful combination. Breeders are as concerned with developing a sweet disposition as they are with the dog's size and coat.

Occasional loose bowels in a puppy generally isn't anything too serious. It can be the result of an upset stomach or a slight cold. Sometimes it will clear up in a day or so without any treatment. If you want to help the puppy's digestion, add some cottage cheese to his diet, or give him a few drops of kaopectate. Instead of tap water, give him barley or oatmeal water (just as you would a human baby). However, if the looseness persists for more than a day or two, a visit to the vet may be required. If the puppy has normal bowel movements alternating with loose bowel movements, it may be a symptom of worms.

If the puppy upchucks a meal or vomits up slime or white froth, it may indicate that his stomach is upset. One good stomach-settler is a pinch of baking soda, or about 8 or 10 drops of pure witch hazel in a teaspoon of cold water two or three times a day. In case of vomiting you should skip a few meals to give the stomach a chance to clear itself out. When you start to

These puppies are not in quarantine. They are fenced off so they are free to run and play safely.

feed him again, give him cooked scraped beef for his first meals and then return to his normal diet. Persistent vomiting may indicate a serious stomach upset or even poisoning and calls for professional help.

WORMING

Practically all puppies start out in life with worms in their insides, either acquired from the mother or picked up in their sleeping quarters. However, there are six different types of worms. Some will be visible in the stool as small white objects; others require microscopic examination of the stool for identification. While there are many commercial worm remedies on the market, it is safest to leave that to your veterinarian, and to follow his instructions on feeding the puppy before and after the worming. If you find that you must administer a worm remedy yourself, read the directions carefully and administer the smallest possible dose. Keep the puppy confined

Facial hairs on the Yorkie are black at birth, mingled with tan. As he reaches maturity, they must become completely tan and not intermingle with any black hairs.

after treatment for worms, since many of the remedies have a strong laxative action and the puppy will soil the house if allowed to roam freely.

THE USEFUL THERMOMETER

Almost every serious puppy ailment shows itself by an increase in the puppy's body temperature. If your little Yorkie acts lifeless, looks dull-eyed and gives an impression of illness, check by using a rectal thermometer. Hold the dog, insert the thermometer which has been lubricated with vaseline and take a reading. The normal temperature is 100.6 to 101.5 (higher than the normal human temperature). Excitement may send it up slightly, but any rise of more than a few points is cause for alarm.

SOME CANINE DISEASES

Many Yorkshires have lived to the age of 20, a ripe old age for any dog, and they are not notably prone to disease. However, you should be familar with the symptoms of some of the more prevalent canine diseases which can strike your dog.

COUGHS, COLDS, BRONCHITIS, PNEUMONIA

Respiratory diseases may affect the Yorkie because he is forced to live in a human rather than a natural doggy environment. Being subjected to a draft or cold after a bath, sleeping near an air conditioner or in the path of air from a fan or near a hot air register or radiator can cause one of these respiratory ailments. The symptoms are similar to those in humans. However, the germs of these diseases are different and do not affect both dogs and humans so that they cannot catch them from each other. Treatment is pretty much the same as for a child with the same illness. Keep the puppy warm, quiet, well fed. Your veterinarian has antibiotics and other remedies to help the pup fight back.

Don't make the common mistake of running your dog to the vet every time he sneezes. If he seems to have a light cold, give him about a quarter of an aspirin tablet and see that he doesn't overexercise himself.

MAJOR DISEASES OF THE DOG

With the proper series of inoculations, your Yorkshire will be almost completely protected against the following canine diseases. However, it occasionally happens that the shot doesn't take and sometimes a different form of the virus appears against which your dog may not be protected.

Rabies: This is an acute disease of the dog's central nervous system and is spread by the bite of an infected animal, the saliva carrying the infection. Rabies occurs in two forms. The first is "Furious Rabies" in which the dog shows a period of melancholy or depression, then irritation, and finally paralysis. The first period lasts from a few hours to several days. During this time, the dog is cross and will try to hide from members of the family. He appears restless and will change his position often. He loses his appetite for food and begins to lick, bite and swallow foreign objects. During the "irritation" phase the dog is spasmodically wild and has impulses to run away. He acts in a fearless manner and runs and bites at everything in sight. If he is caged or confined he will fight at the bars, often breaking teeth or fracturing his jaw. His bark becomes a peculiar howl. In the final or paralysis stage, the animal's lower jaw becomes paralyzed and hangs down; he walks with a stagger and saliva drips from his mouth. Within four to eight days after the onset of paralysis, the dog dies.

The second form of rabies, "Dumb Rabies," is characterized by the dog's walking in a bear-like manner with his head down. The lower jaw is paralyzed and the dog is unable to bite. Outwardly it may seem as though he has a bone caught in his throat.

Even if your Yorkie should be bitten by a rabid dog or other animal, he can probably be saved if you get him to the vet in time for a series of injections. However, by the time the symptoms appear the disease is so far advanced that no cure is possible. But remember that an annual rabies inoculation is almost certain protection against rabies.

Distemper: Young dogs are most susceptible to distemper, although it may affect dogs of all ages. The dog will lose his appetite, seem depressed, chilled, and run a fever. Often he will have a watery discharge from his eyes and nose. Unless treated promptly, the disease goes into advanced stages with infections of the lungs, intestines and nervous system, and dogs that recover may be left with some impairment such as a twitch or other nervous mannerism. The best protection against this is very early inoculation — preferably even before the puppy is old enough to go out into the street and meet other dogs.

Hepatitis: Veterinarians report an increase in the spread of this virus disease in recent years, usually with younger dogs as the victims. The initial symptoms — drowsiness, vomiting, great thirst, loss of appetite and a high temperature — closely resemble distemper. These symptoms are often accompanied by swellings on the head, neck and lower parts of the belly. The disease strikes quickly and death may occur in a few hours. Protection is afforded by injection with a new vaccine.

Leptospirosis: This disease is caused by bacteria which live in stagnant or slow-moving water. It is carried by rats and dogs, and many dogs are believed to get it from licking the urine or feces of infected rats. The symptoms are increased thirst, depression and weakness. In the acute stage, there is vomiting, diarrhea and a brown discoloration of the jaws, tongue and teeth, caused by an inflammation of the kidneys. This disease can be cured if caught in time, but it is best to ward it off with a vaccine which your vet can administer along with the distemper shots.

External Parasites: The Yorkshire needs special care in regard to fleas, ticks or lice. Scratching at the irritation caused by these pests can ruin the dog's coat. The dog that is groomed regularly and provided with clean sleeping quarters should not have much trouble on this score. However, it would be a wise precaution to spray his sleeping quarters occasionally with an anti-parasite powder that you can get at your pet shop or from your vet. For the dog himself, because of his luxuriant coat, a liquid spray would probably be more effective than a powder. If the dog is out of doors during the tick season he should be treated with a dip-bath.

Skin Ailments: It may be difficult to spot skin disorders on your longhaired Yorkshire, but any persistent scratching may indicate an irritation, and whenever you groom him, look for the reddish spots that may indicate eczema or some rash or fungus infection. Rather than self-treatment, take him to the veterinarian as some of the conditions may be difficult to eradicate and can cause permanent harm to his coat.

Above all, don't be grim about the lessons. Take time out for a little affectionate play.

The Yorkie's keen attention to moving objects makes him a captive audience whether or not the thing is within his reach.

THE FEMALE PUPPY

If you want to spay your female you can have it done while she is still a puppy. She may be spayed before her first seasonal period or you may breed her and still spay her afterward.

The first sign of the female's being in season is a thin red discharge, which will increase for about a week, when it changes color to a thin yellowish stain, lasting about another week. Simultaneously there is a swelling of the vulva, the dog's external sexual organ. The second week is the crucial period, when she could be bred if you want her to have puppies, but it is possible for the period to be shorter or longer, so it is best not to take unnecessary risks at any time. After a third week the swelling decreases and the period is over.

If you have an absolutely climb-proof and dig-proof run within your yard, it will be safe to leave her there, but otherwise the female in season should be shut indoors. Don't leave her out alone for even a minute; she should be exercised only on leash. If you want to prevent the neighborhood dogs from hanging around your doorstep, as they inevitably will as soon as they discover that your female is in season, take her some distance away from the house before you let her relieve herself. Take her in your car to a park or field for a chance to stretch her legs. After three weeks are up you can let her out as before, with no worry that she can have puppies until the next season. But if you want to have her spayed, consult your veterinarian about the time and age at which he prefers to do it. With a young dog the operation is simple and after a night or two at the animal hospital she can be at home, wearing only a small bandage as a souvenir.

4. Housebreaking and Training Your Yorkshire

HE'S A TERRIER

When you housebreak and train your Yorkshire Terrier you must keep in mind that he's a Terrier — aggressive, spunky, courageous, self-willed, independent. You have to show him from the start who's boss.

PAPER TRAINING

A dog has a natural instinct to avoid soiling the place where he sleeps. Utilize that instinct in paper training your Yorkie. When you notice him squatting or running around in a little, agitated circle, or sniffing the papers, take him over to the place that you want to serve as his "toilet" and hold him there till he does his business. When he does, praise him, telling him what a good dog he is. When he makes a mistake, scold him severely. By a combination of praise when he does what you want, scolding when he doesn't, your dog will get the idea of paper training in a surprisingly short time. When you pick up soiled papers, it helps to leave some damp sheets down so that his nose will guide him back to the spot.

If you want to take advantage of modern science you can get two liquids at your pet shop. One will encourage the puppy to use a certain area; the other will keep him away from the place that is sprinkled or sprayed with the solution.

Don't let the small size of the Yorkshire induce you to treat him like an infant. The little Yorkie is tough and you have to be tougher to train him. After he has been shown what's expected in his paper training, get tough when he misbehaves. Hold his nose close to the mess he has made and cuff him sharply on the nose or slap his rear end.

Curb training, the next step in housebreaking, has to wait until the pup is a little older and has learned to walk on a leash.

PUPPY DISCIPLINE

A lot of people who have never had a dog will deliver long lectures on the subject of "never hit a dog." They'll tell you that the puppy that has been slapped will grow into a hand-shy, cowering dog. That's just not so. A dog, even a young one, will not resent correction when it's deserved. But you must correct him properly. Never chase the dog, slapping at him with a paper or your hand. Keep calm, catch the puppy, hold him firmly, and administer the necessary "spanking." Dogs, especially young pups, do not like loud noises. A clap of the hands, slamming down a paper or book, and a loud "NO" at the same time will soon teach your Yorkie pup the meaning of the word "No." At the same time, let him connect some other word or expression with a favorable act. "Good dog," "good girl" or a similar phrase in an approving tone of voice — and dogs are very sensitive to tones of the human voice — will help the learning process.

CHEWING

All puppies will be destructive. Chewing and tasting things is the way a puppy becomes acquainted with the physical world around him, and the

Children should realize that puppies are delicate. They can have plenty of fun without playing roughly.

Born with an abundance of black hair on face and head, the Yorkie's facial hair turns to rich golden tan as he matures. In fact, the Yorkshire standard disallows any black hairs to be intermingled with the tan on the head.

young puppy will chew almost anything in the hope that it may be tasty and digestible. As soon as the puppy has learned the word "No" it can be used to curb his chewing habits. Watch the young dog carefully. When he approaches anything "verboten" order him to leave it alone. If he disobeys, correct him immediately. At the same time, give him some chewable toys of his own. Your pet shop will have a good selection, but be careful to choose toys that are made of leather or hard rubber. Avoid the soft rubber toys that the dog can chew into swallowable pieces. If you give him household things to play with, be sensible in your selection. If you give the puppy a slipper he will find it hard to distinguish between the slipper that is his toy and the one that you just got as a Christmas gift. During his early puppyhood never leave the Yorkie alone and free to roam about the house. Keep him confined to his own area for the first two months or so. If you stop him from developing bad habits as a puppy, he will more easily grow into a civilized member of your family. If you come back and find something that has been chewed up some hours before, don't bother to correct your dog for that misstep. To have any real value, a correction must be administered immediately after the offense. Otherwise the puppy won't know why he is being punished. Showing him something that he chewed two hours before and bawling him out for it has no meaning to him.

BARKING

Small dogs are characteristically "yappy." Perhaps they try to make up in sound what they lack in size, but with patience and persistence you can get your Yorkie to keep quiet even when he's left alone in the house or when a visitor rings the doorbell or the milkman comes.

Show the puppy from the start that you consider excessive barking an anti-social act. When he barks, grab his muzzle, hold his mouth closed and give him a firm command to stop. Above all, do not show him by your attitude that barking is "cute" sometimes, and then reprimand him for barking at another time. When the puppy barks, make a louder noise than he can and shout "No." When he finds that his bark brings an unpleasant and slightly frightening reaction, he'll stop barking.

Teaching the dog not to bark when he's left alone in the house calls for the application of canine psychology. Leave him alone in a room. When he barks, go back into the room and reprimand him severely, then step out again and wait by the door. He may bark as soon as he thinks you're gone. When that happens, pound the door with your fist and order him to stop. And don't think that training a dog not to bark will break his spirit.

Training the Yorkie not to bark at other dogs will take a bit of work on your part. The Yorkshire straining at his leash and barking his head off at a big Boxer or Collie makes a delightful picture, but it gets annoying if it goes on year after year. Be firm from the start. At the first sign of a bark at another dog, grab his muzzle and order him to stop. If he persists you can make a no-bark muzzle by taking a piece of gauze bandage, running it around his muzzle and under his jaws and knotting it around his neck. When you put it on, make it clear to the dog that it's being done because he's barking. After a few minutes take it off but put it back on if he barks again. He'll soon learn that barking gets his nose tied up and not-barking doesn't.

CLIMBING ON FURNITURE

Despite his short legs, your Yorkie may show a surprising ability to climb onto upholstered furniture. The upholstery holds the scent of the people he likes, and besides, it's more comfortable than the hard floor or even the carpet. Sometimes verbal corrections will be enough to establish the fact that the furniture is taboo. If not, try putting crinkly cellophane on the furniture to keep him off. If that doesn't work, you can get liquids at your pet store that you can't smell, but whose odor keeps the dog off. Another good trick is the mousetrap surprise. Put a small unbaited but set mousetrap on the piece of furniture that your Yorkshire chooses for his naps. Once he's surprised by the snap of the trap, he'll keep away from that spot. You can put the trap under a piece of paper or cloth if you're afraid that it may hurt the dog, or you may even find a child's toy that snaps which will serve the same purpose as the mousetrap.

THE TOO-FRIENDLY PUPPY

Your Yorkie will probably like people and will try to show his liking for them by trying to climb all over anyone he meets. This may be another "cute" act, but if you're planning to show your dog, you won't want him climbing all over the judge in the ring. Besides, not all your friends and relatives are dog lovers and many people prefer to admire dogs from a slight distance. Curbing the puppy's desire to scramble over people will require cooperation from others. Instruct your friends to give the puppy a slight kick or slap when he gets overattentive, but then have them call him back and pet him to show that people aren't hostile.

And here's a tip on petting the puppy. If everyone pets him on top of the head, as most people do, he may develop the habit of coming over to people with his head down to receive his due. Instead, he should be chucked under the chin. That will keep him in an attractive head-up pose when he greets people — and improve his posture in the show ring or on the street.

KIDS IN THE FAMILY

If there are young children in the family, you may have to train them a bit while you are training the Yorkshire puppy. Don't allow the kids to get the young puppy overexcited, and try to impress them with the importance of doing their share in training him, but don't become overly strict. Children, and puppies alike must have fun as they are learning to develop properly. However, instruct the children not to play tug-of-war with the Yorkie puppy.

The Yorkshire's coat, his most outstanding characteristic, needs a great deal of care. Before you begin to brush him, spray his coat with dressing.

This game can pull the pup's teeth out of line. There are plenty of other games that the kids and the puppy can enjoy.

WALKING ON LEAD

Now comes another battle of wills, when you train your Yorkshire to walk at the end of his leash — what the "doggy" people always call the "lead." For the Yorkie, the best type is the thin, nylon lead with a slip-noose collar arrangement that is called a show lead. This type of leash will give you enough control over the dog to manage him and it won't destroy the attractive whiskers and fall that give the Yorkie his distinctive appearance.

First give the puppy a chance to get acquainted with the lead and collar. Slip the collar around his neck and let the lead dangle on the floor

Just show your pet who's walking whom and he'll become a gay street companion. Hold the lead in your right hand; use your left to give sharp jerks when correction is needed.

and let him play with it for a while to get the feel of it. Then pick up the end of the lead and call the dog over to you, giving the lead gentle jerks to get across the idea that he should move with the lead. You can expect a battle royal at first, as the Yorkie isn't giving up his freedom to roam without putting up a good fight. But lead-training is the basis of all further training, so you have to be firm enough to win.

When you begin walking him outdoors you can expect him to pull back with all his strength, plant his hindquarters on the pavement or try to run in circles around you.

There are two important tricks in training the dog to follow the lead. First, do not pull the dog. Instead, use the lead to give *sharp jerks* and then release the pressure. The dog soon learns that if he follows the path of least resistance, his walks are pleasanter. Second, walk *fast* when you are training the dog to follow the lead. Walking at a brisk pace forces the dog to follow you; walking slowly gives him too much opportunity for antics of his own.

Use surprise tactics. If the dog runs to the end of the lead to bark at another dog, reverse your course sharply, giving the lead a snap to pull the dog back with you. You won't hurt him. However, limit the length of your first walks to a few minutes each. Another good idea is to carry the puppy a distance away from home and then put him down and start walking back home. Many young dogs are better at coming than they are at going. Keep the puppy at your left side when you are walking him. Hold the lead in your right hand, using your left hand to snap the lead for corrections. Keep up a running chain of conversation with the dog while he is on lead to keep his attention focused on you.

CURB TRAINING THE YORKIE

As soon as your Yorkie begins to get the idea of the lead, you can begin his curb training, which is essential for a city dog. Assuming that his paper training is progressing, you can cut down the area of paper in his living quarters and show him that using the curb is acceptable. When he shows by sniffing the floor or otherwise that he has to "go," pick him up and carry him out to the street. Put him down in the curb and walk him slowly back and forth, pushing him back if he tries to climb up on the sidewalk and encouraging him with words to do his stuff. Usually he will leave a puddle and then nothing. It may help if you can find a piece of paper in the curb and stand him over it while urging him on. At this stage of training, some people use baby-sized glycerine suppositories to bring faster reaction. Each time the puppy does something in the right place, praise him lavishly. Remember that a young puppy requires many, many trips outdoors daily. He should be taken out immediately on waking in the morning, after each meal, after every period of active exercise and last thing in the evening. It will help in this training if you gradually cut down the liquid content of his late afternoon meal.

5. Basic Obedience Training for the Yorkshire

The purpose of obedience training is not to turn your dog into a puppet — you can be sure this won't happen to your spirited Yorkie — but to make him a civilized member of the community in which he will live, and to keep him safe. As soon as your dog has been housebroken and has learned to walk fairly well on lead, you can gradually begin his more formal training. This training is most important as it makes the difference between having an undisciplined animal in the house or having an enjoyable companion. Both you and your dog will learn a lot from training.

TRAINING TO SIT

Training your dog to sit should be fairly easy. Stand him on your left side, holding the lead fairly short, and command him to "Sit." As you give the verbal command, pull up slightly with the lead and push his hindquarters down (you may have to kneel to do this). Do not let him lie down or stand up. Keep him in a sitting position for a moment, then release the pressure on the lead and praise him. Your Yorkie, having a mind of his own, may resent being told when to sit and may put up a bit of a fuss, but don't let him get away with any nonsense. If he attempts to bite, slap him sharply across the nose. If he squirms and tries to get away, then take a few steps forward and try making him sit again. Constantly repeat the command word as you hold him in a sitting position, thus fitting the word to the action in his mind. After a while, he will begin to get the idea and will sit without your having to push his back down. When he reaches that stage, insist that he sit on command. If he is slow to obey, slap his hindquarters with the end of the lead to get him down fast. Teach him to sit on command facing you as well as when he is at your side. When he begins sitting on command with the lead on, try it with the lead off.

If you want your Yorkie to sit and stay, pull up slightly on the lead with your left hand and give the hand signal with your right. While he's still learning, use the verbal command too. Remember that repetition is the basis for all learning.

THE "LIE DOWN"

The object of this is to get the dog to lie down either on the verbal command "Down!" or when you give him a hand signal, your hand raised, palm toward the dog — a sort of threatening gesture.

Don't start this until the dog is almost letter-perfect in sitting on command. Then, place the dog in a sit. Force him down by pulling his front feet out forward while pressing on his shoulders and repeating "Down!" Hold the dog down and stroke him gently to let him know that staying down is what you expect of him.

After he begins to get the idea, slide the lead under your left foot and give the command "Down!" At the same time, pull on the lead. This will help get the dog down. Meanwhile, raise your left hand in the down signal. Don't expect to accomplish all this in one session. Be patient and work with the dog. He'll cooperate if you show him just what you expect him to do.

THE "STAY"

The next step is to train your Yorkie to stay put in either a "sit" or "down" position. Sit him at your side. Give him the command "Stay," but be careful not to use his name with that command as hearing his name may lead him to think that some action is expected of him. If he begins to move, repeat "Stay" firmly and hold him down in the sit. Constantly repeat the word "stay" to fix the meaning of that command in his mind. When he stays for a short time, gradually increase the length of his stay. The hand signal for "stay" is a downward sweep of your hand toward the dog's nose, with the palm toward him. While he is sitting, walk around him and stand in front of him. Hold the lead at first; later, drop the lead on the ground in front of him and keep him sitting. If he bolts, correct him severely and force him back to a sit in the same place.

Use some word such as "okay" or "up" to let him know when he can get up, and praise him well for a good performance. As this practice continues, walk farther and farther away from him. Later, try sitting him, giving him the command to stay, and then walk out of sight, first for a few seconds, then

To help your dog get the idea of "Down!" slide the lead under your foot and pull up on it as you give the verbal command. Soon he'll learn to respond to a hand signal alone.

for longer periods. A well-trained dog should stay where you put him without moving for three minutes or more.

Similarly, practice having him stay in down position, first with you near him, later when you step out of sight.

THE "COME" ON COMMAND

A young puppy will come a-running to people, but an older puppy or dog will have other plans of his own when his master calls him. However, you can train your Yorkie to come when you call him if you begin when he is young. At first, work with him on lead. Sit the dog, then back away the length of the lead and call him, putting as much coaxing affection in your voice as possible. Give an easy tug on the lead to get him started. When he does come, make a big fuss over him and it might help to hand him a piece of dog candy or food as a reward. He should get the idea soon. Then attach a long piece of cord to the lead — 15 or 20 feet — and make him come to you from that distance. When he's coming pretty consistently, have him sit when he reaches you.

Don't be too eager to practice coming on command off lead. Wait till you are certain that you have the dog under perfect control before you try calling him when he's free. Once he gets the idea that he can disobey a command to come and get away with it, your training program will suffer a serious setback. Keep in mind that your dog's life may depend on his immediate response to a command to come when he is called. If he disobeys off lead, put the collar back on and correct him severely with jerks of the lead. He'll get the idea.

In training your dog to come, never use the command when you want to punish him. He should associate the "come" with something pleasant. If he comes very slowly, you can speed his response by pulling on the lead, calling him and running backward with him at a brisk pace.

At first, practice the "sit," "down," "stay" and "come" indoors; then try it in an outdoor area where there are distractions to show the dog that he must obey under any conditions.

HEELING

"Heeling" in dog language means having your pet walk alongside you on your left side, close to your left leg, on lead or off. With patience and effort you can train your Yorkie to walk with you even on a crowded street or in the presence of other dogs. However, don't begin this part of his training too early. Normally a dog much under six months old is just too young to absorb the idea of heeling — although there are exceptions and your Yorkie may be precocious.

For training him to heel, you may have to substitute a metal-link "choke" collar for the nylon lead that you have been using. Be certain to learn the correct way to put on this collar so that the loop which attaches to the lead goes *over*, not *under* the dog's neck. When you jerk on the lead it will

When your Yorkie comes on command, make a big fuss over him and perhaps reward him with a treat.

tighten, when you release pressure it will loosen.

With enough repetition, your dog will associate the word "heel" with your desire to have him at your left leg. The tool for this part of the training is the lead and collar, assisted by your verbal commands.

Put the dog at your left side, sitting. Then say "heel" loudly and start walking at a brisk pace. Do not pull the dog with you, but guide him by tugs at the lead. Keep some slack on the lead and use your left hand to snap the lead for a correction. Always start off with your left foot and after a while the dog will learn to watch that foot and follow it. Keep repeating "heel" as you walk, snapping the dog back into position if he lags behind or forges ahead. If he gets out of control, reverse your course sharply and

Today's Yorkie, although smaller, is remarkably like the first members of the breed developed a century ago.

snap him along after you. Keep up a running conversation with your dog, telling him what a good fellow he is when he is heeling, letting him know when he is not.

At first limit your heeling practice to about 5 minutes at a time; later extend it to 15 minutes or a half-hour. To keep your dog interested, vary the routine. Make right and left turns, change your pace from a normal walk to a fast trot to a very slow walk. Occasionally make a sharp about-face.

Remember to emphasize the word "heel" throughout this practice and to use your voice to let him know that you are displeased when he goes ahead or drops behind or swings wide.

If you are handling him properly, the Yorkie should begin to get the idea of heeling in about 15 minutes. If you get no response whatever, if the dog runs away from you, fights the lead, gets you and himself tangled in the lead, it may indicate that he is still young, or that you aren't showing him what you expect him to do.

Practicing 15 minutes a day, in 6 or 7 weeks your Yorkie should have developed to the stage where you can remove the lead and he'll heel alongside you. First try throwing the lead over your shoulder or fastening it to your belt, or remove the lead and tie a piece of thin cord (fishing line will do nicely) to his collar. Then try him off lead. Keep his attention by constantly talking; slap your left leg to keep his attention on you. If he breaks away, return to the collar and lead treatment for a while.

"HEEL" MEANS SIT, TOO

To the dog, the command "Heel" will also mean that he has to sit in heel position at your left side when you stop walking — with no additional command from you. As you practice heeling, force him to sit whenever you stop, at first using the word "sit," then switching over to the command "heel." He'll soon get the idea and plop his rear end down when you stop and wait for you to give the command "heel" and start walking again.

Teach your dog to stand on a table. He'll have to do plenty of it when he is being groomed or examined by the vet.

When you stop walking, your dog should automatically sit and stay.

To teach the dog to come to heel position when you are standing still, sit him in front of you. Give the command, then swing him around to your left side and sit him, repeating "heel." It will help if you take a step forward as you swing him, which will give him room to maneuver his backside. From the start, try to get him to sit facing forward, not at an angle.

A REVIEW

Your Yorkie's basic training should have taught him to sit and lie down on command, to stay on your order, to heel on and off lead. How long should it take? That depends largely on how good a teacher you are and how consistently you work with your dog. In most dog-training schools where the handler works with the dog one evening a week and promises to practice for 15 minutes to a half-hour each evening, about 10 weeks is allowed for this training. Dogs are usually expected to be about 6 months old before they are accepted for schooling.

If you can attend training classes with your Yorkie you'll find the teaching-learning process more fun for you and your dog. Many of the Yorkshire Terrier clubs have set up obedience classes; in many cities the A.S.P.C.A. has training classes and there are obedience training clubs throughout the country.

A well-trained dog will give you a great deal of pleasure. You can both be proud of your accomplishments.

In spite of his smallness of stature, the Yorkie's intelligence and game attitude have made him a successful competitor in an increasing number of advanced obedience trials in recent years.

ADVANCED TRAINING AND OBEDIENCE TRIALS

In recent years, many Yorkshire Terrier owners have found that their dogs show considerable aptitude for advanced obedience training and the number of Yorkies entered in obedience trials at A.K.C. shows has been increasing. Most dog shows now include obedience classes at which your dog can qualify for his "degrees" to demonstrate his usefulness as a companion dog, not merely as a pet or show dog.

The A.K.C. obedience trials are divided into three classes: Novice, Open and Utility.

In the Novice Class, the dog will be judged on the following basis:

Test	Maximum Score
Heel on leash	35
Stand for examination by judge	30
Heel free—off leash	45
Recall (come on command)	30
1-minute sit	30
3-minute down	30
Maximum total score	200

If the dog "qualifies" in three different shows by earning at least 50 per cent of the points for each test, with a total of at least 170 for the trial, he has earned the Companion Dog degree and the letters C.D. are entered in the stud book after his name.

After the dog has qualified as a C.D., he is eligible to enter the Open Class competition where he will be judged on this basis:

Test	Maximum Score
Heel free	40
Drop on recall	30
Retrieve (wooden dumbbell) on flat	25
Retrieve over obstacle (hurdle)	35
Broad jump	20
3-minute sit	25
5-minute down	25
Maximum total score	200

Again he must qualify in three shows for the C.D.X. (Companion Dog Excellent) title and then is eligible for the Utility Class where he can earn the Utility Dog degree in these rugged tests:

Test	Maximum Score
Scent discrimination (picking up article handled by master from group of articles) — Article #1	20
Scent discrimination—Article #2	20
Scent discrimination — Article #3	20
Seek back (picking up article dropped by handler)	30
Signal exercise (heeling, etc., on hand signal only)	35
Directed jumping (over hurdle and bar jump)	40
Group examination	35
Maximum total score	200

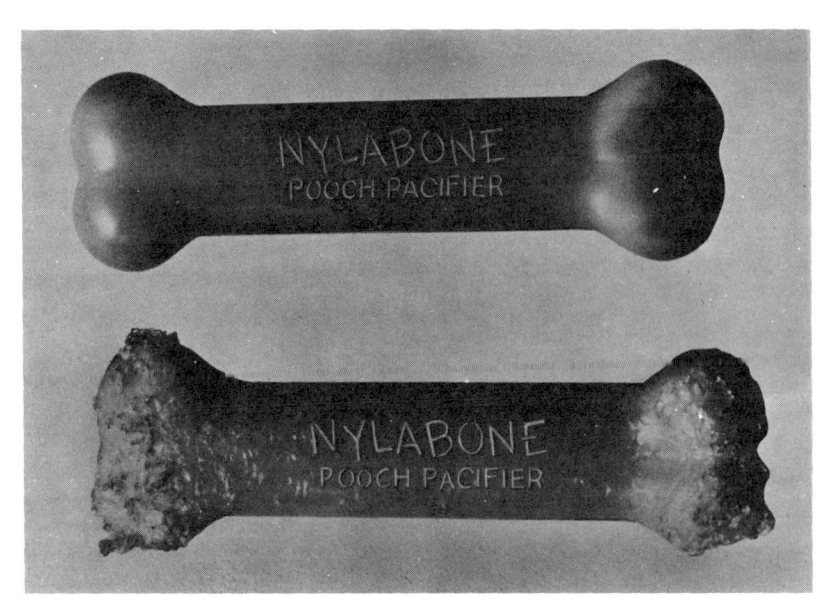

NYLABONE® is a necessity that is available at your local petshop (not in supermarkets). The puppy or grown dog chews the hambone flavored nylon into a frilly dog toothbrush, massaging his gums and cleaning his teeth as he plays. Veterinarians highly recommend this product . . . but beware of cheap imitations which might splinter or break.

Besides the formal A.K.C. obedience trials, there are informal "match" shows in which dogs compete for ribbons and inexpensive trophies. These shows are run by local Yorkshire clubs and by all-breed obedience clubs, and in many localities the A.S.P.C.A. and other groups conduct their own obedience shows. Your local pet shop or kennel can keep you informed about such shows in your vicinity and you will find them listed in the different dog magazines or in the pet column of your local paper.

The best training for advanced obedience routines is a dog school or experienced dog trainer, but you can get a lot of training tips in HOW TO HOUSEBREAK AND TRAIN YOUR DOG, by Arthur Liebers, a Sterling-TFH book.

6. Grooming the Yorkshire Terrier

THE COAT

The Yorkshire's coat is his most important characteristic, and the desirable long, silky coat requires constant care. It is necessary to start grooming the puppy at the age of three months, while his coat is still undeveloped. Accustom your young dog to standing on a table for his grooming sessions. If you break him in properly, he will not mind being handled and groomed later. The coat should be brushed every day with a stiff bristle brush. Before brushing, spray the coat with a little coat dressing as the hairs are brittle when dry and may have a tendency to break. Pet shops also have a heavy oil which is excellent for keeping the Yorkie's hair from matting, or if some mats develop, they can be brushed out when impregnated with this oil.

If you want to develop your dog's coat to the peak of show perfection, tie the clumps of hair in little wax papers. Separate the hair in small folds, put wax paper around the folds, and make little packets of hair. Keep these packets loose as tight tying will harm the coat. It might be a good idea to have the breeder who sells you your Yorkie show you how to do this with an adult dog.

Normal brushing and care will give your Yorkie a good coat even if you do not go to the extreme of wrapping his hairs, but for a show dog this is a "must." Unlike most other breeds, the Yorkie requires frequent bathing — at least twice a month — but be sure to use a shampoo with a lanolin base as the bathings will otherwise dry out his coat and remove the oils from his skin.

When drying your Yorkie after his bath be careful not to rub his coat vigorously, but be gentle and pat the coat dry and then brush. You'll find it worth-while to use a hair-dryer to speed up the drying after the bath. A dryer on a stand is best, although the portable dryer will do an effective job. The dryer not only reduces the possibility of your dog's catching cold after a bath, but also helps keep his coat fluffy.

Daily brushing and bi-weekly bathing will help your Yorkie develop his coat. Never trim the Yorkie, but cut the hair on his ears as its weight

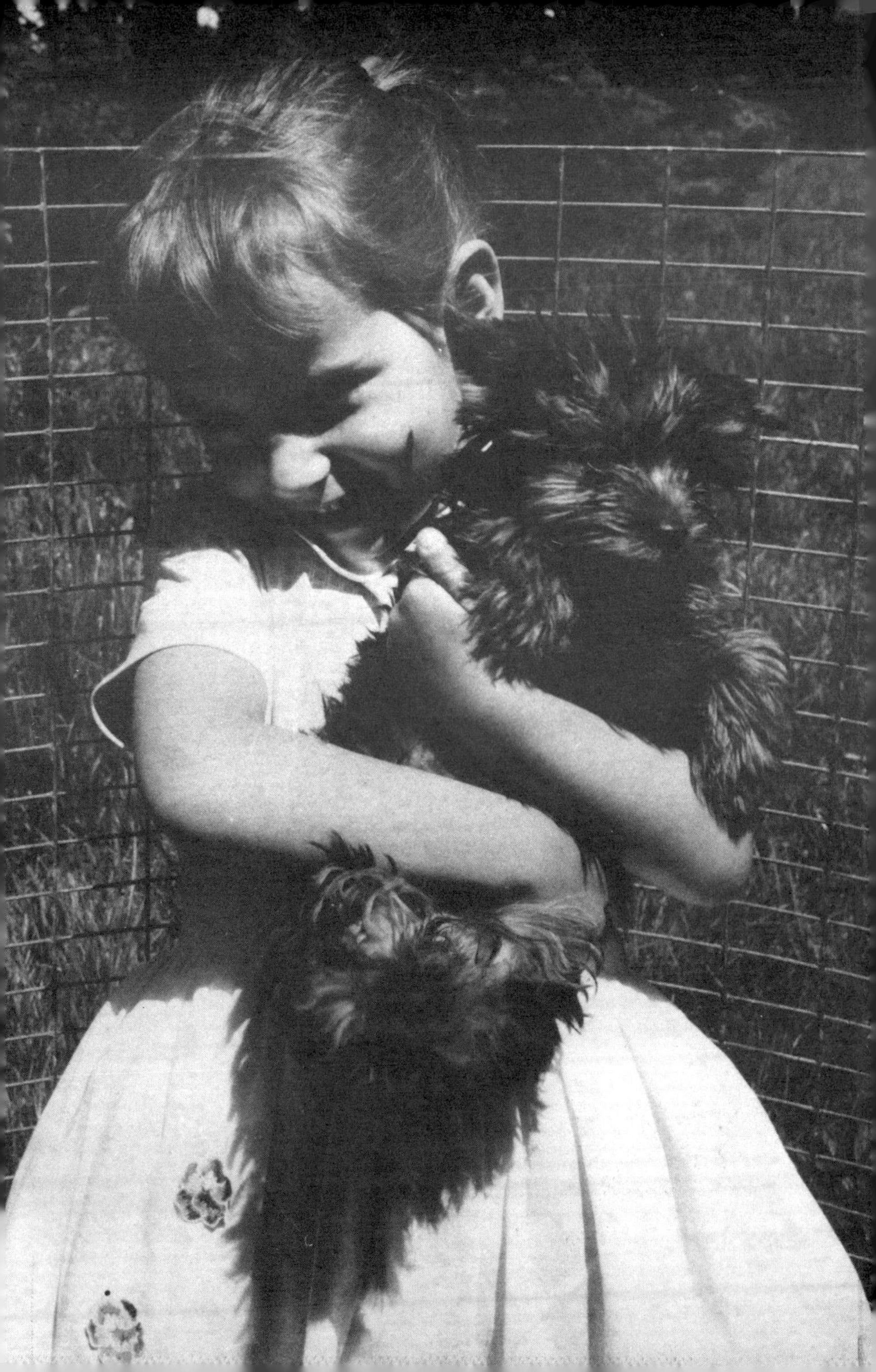

Although the wicker carrying case looks like a comfortable bed, puppies will try to chew it. Use an old blanket instead.

The Yorkie puppy will outgrow the bedraggled look in a few months and develop the long, beautiful adult coat that is associated with the breed.

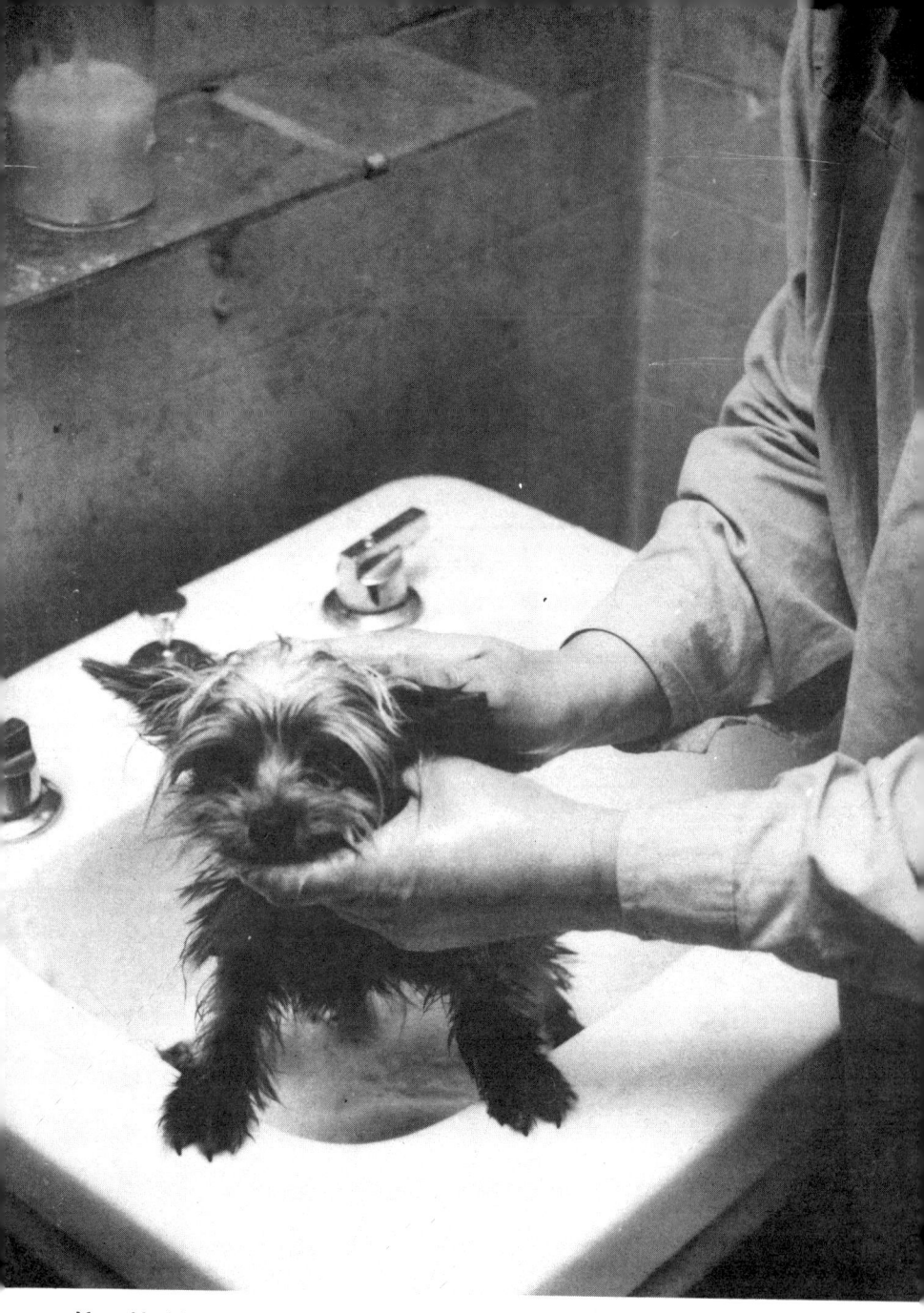

Your Yorkie will need a bath at least twice a month. Use a shampoo with a lanolin base so his coat isn't dried out.

may make his ears droop. You don't want your Yorkie to look like a miniature Old English Sheep Dog, so keep the hair off his eyes by pulling it back and tying it in place with a ribbon or rubber band topknot. The back should have a part in it running down the middle and the hair should fall down straight on either side. (Colors range from dark slate to silver-blue, but the present show standards prefer the steel blue with deep golden tan on the face and legs.)

Be sure your pet is completely dry after his bath, but don't rub his coat vigorously. Pat it dry gently with a warm towel. A hair dryer is an even better idea. Afterwards spray him to replace the oils in his coat and skin.

When giving a pill to your Yorkie, tilt back the head and insert the pill far back into the mouth to make swallowing easy. When you visit the vet, have him check the dog's teeth for tartar build-up. You can remove tartar yourself with a tooth scraper, but have the veterinarian instruct you in its proper use.

OTHER CARE

As the Yorkie probably won't do too much running on rough ground, you'll have to have his toenails trimmed occasionally, and this is a job that's best done by a professional groomer or a vet. Otherwise there's too much danger of cutting into the blood vessels in the dog's nails. Periodically, clean out his ears with a cotton swab dipped into ether or alcohol.

One of the problems of Yorkies is their teeth. Don't be alarmed if you find two sets of teeth in your puppy's mouth, as this happens sometimes. Have your vet extract the excess teeth so that the permanent teeth will grow naturally and not crooked. Yorkies' teeth often have a tendency to discolor, so have your vet check them whenever you have reason to visit him.

Toenail trimming needs a professional hand, but your vet can show you how to use the special dog clippers.

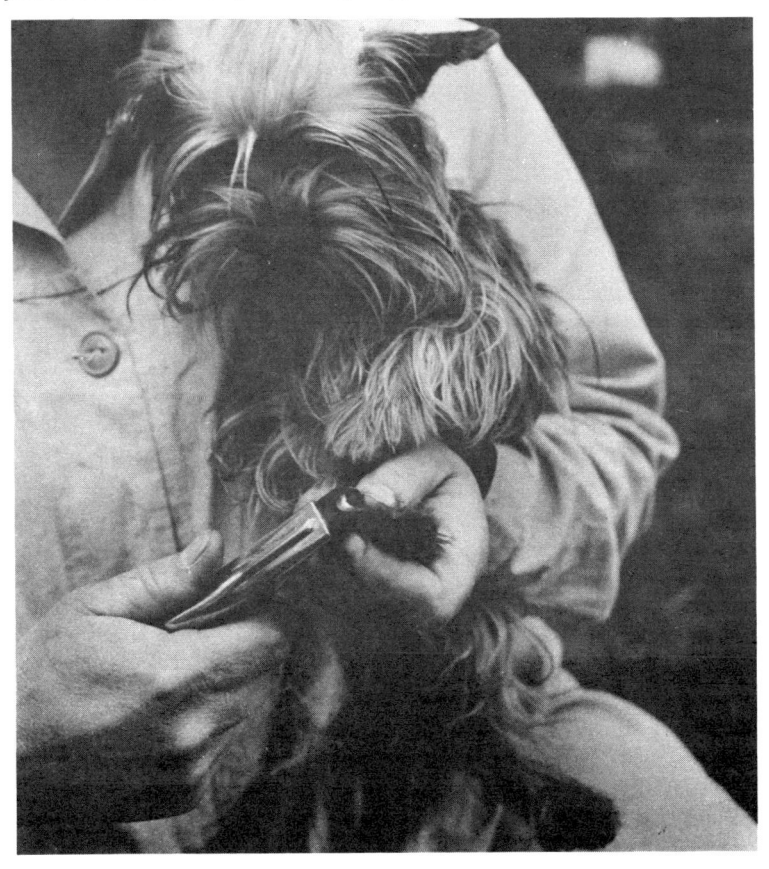

THE COAT TAKES TIME

As we mentioned earlier, it's hard to tell how the coat of a Yorkie will develop. Most Yorkies develop good coats only after a year and sometimes it takes as long as two years — even with care — before the dog blossoms into the lovely creature that has captivated the toy-dog fanciers. Quite often a puppy with the worst coat in the litter develops into the best-coated adult dog. Because the coat is so important in judging this breed, it is generally almost impossible to even guess at the Yorkie's show potential until he is at least 10 months old.

(Below) Your Yorkie's beauty treatment starts with coat dressing sprayed on to protect the brittle hairs.

(Opposite page, above) Then brush him with a stiff bristle brush.

(Opposite page, below) The next step is wrapping the coat in waxed or florist's paper. Ask a Yorkshire breeder to show you how.

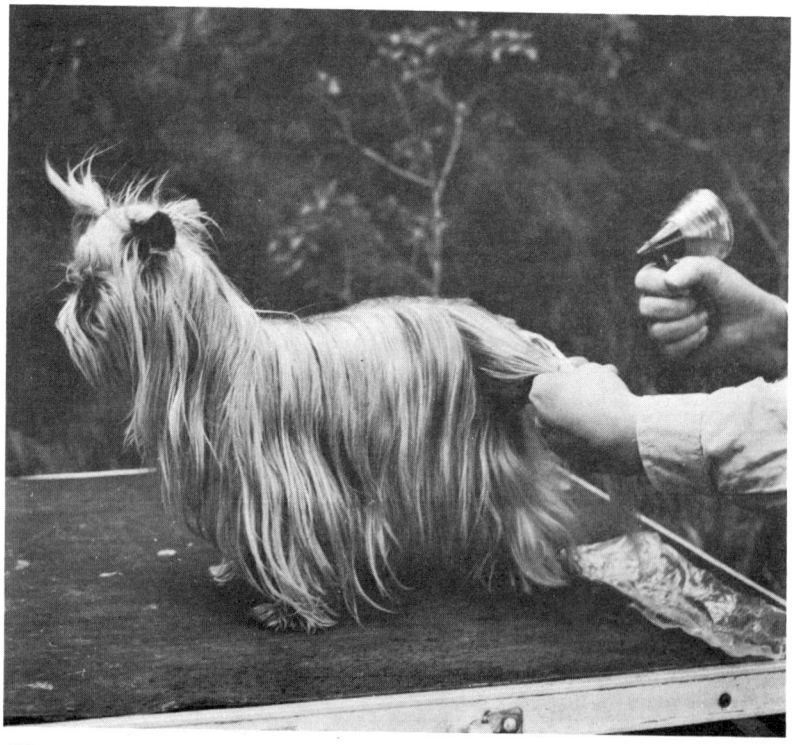

51

JUDGES' SCORING CHART

	Points
Formation and Terrier Appearance	15
Color of Hair on Body	15
Richness of Tan on Head and Legs	15
Quality and Texture of Coat	10
Quality and Length of Coat	10
Head	10
Mouth	5
Legs and Feet	5
Ears	5
Eyes	5
Carriage of Tail	5
Total	100

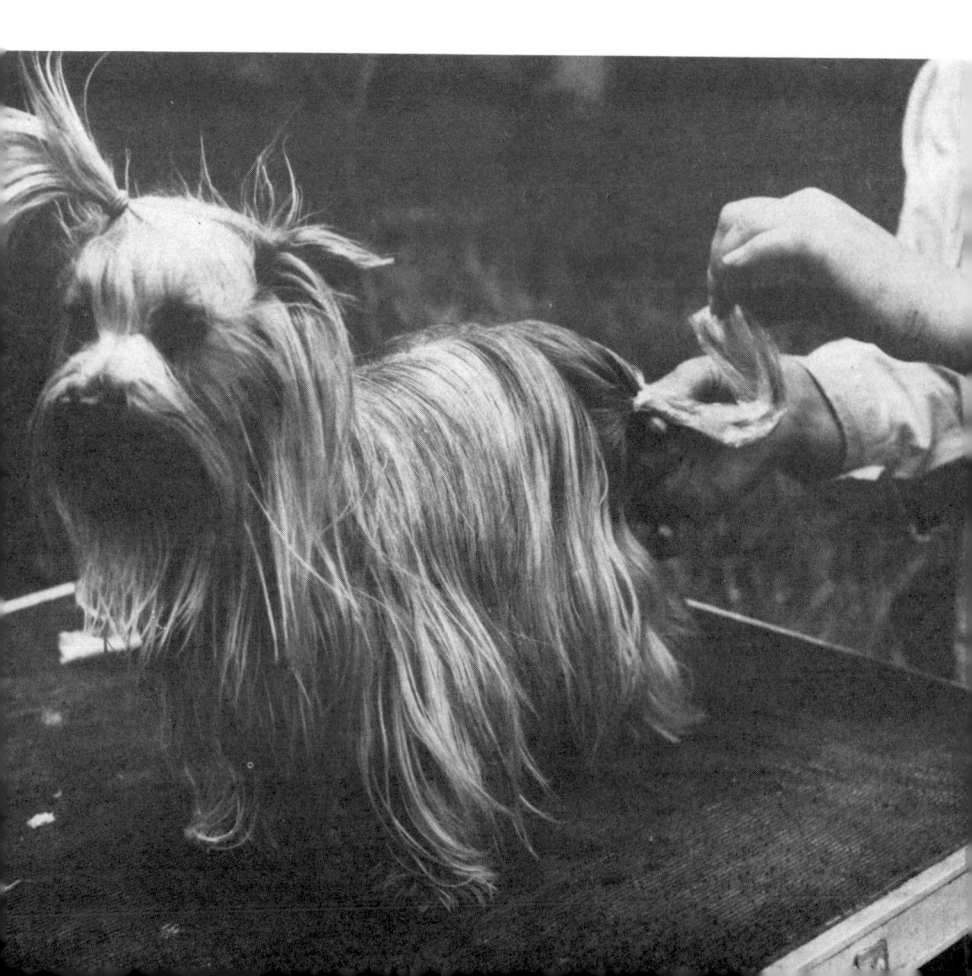

Keep the packets of hair loose. Your Yorkie won't mind spending the day with his hair "set."

If your Yorkie gets used to grooming at an early age, he will stand quietly and enjoy the attention. Be careful that you do not pinch their skin when tying the hair.

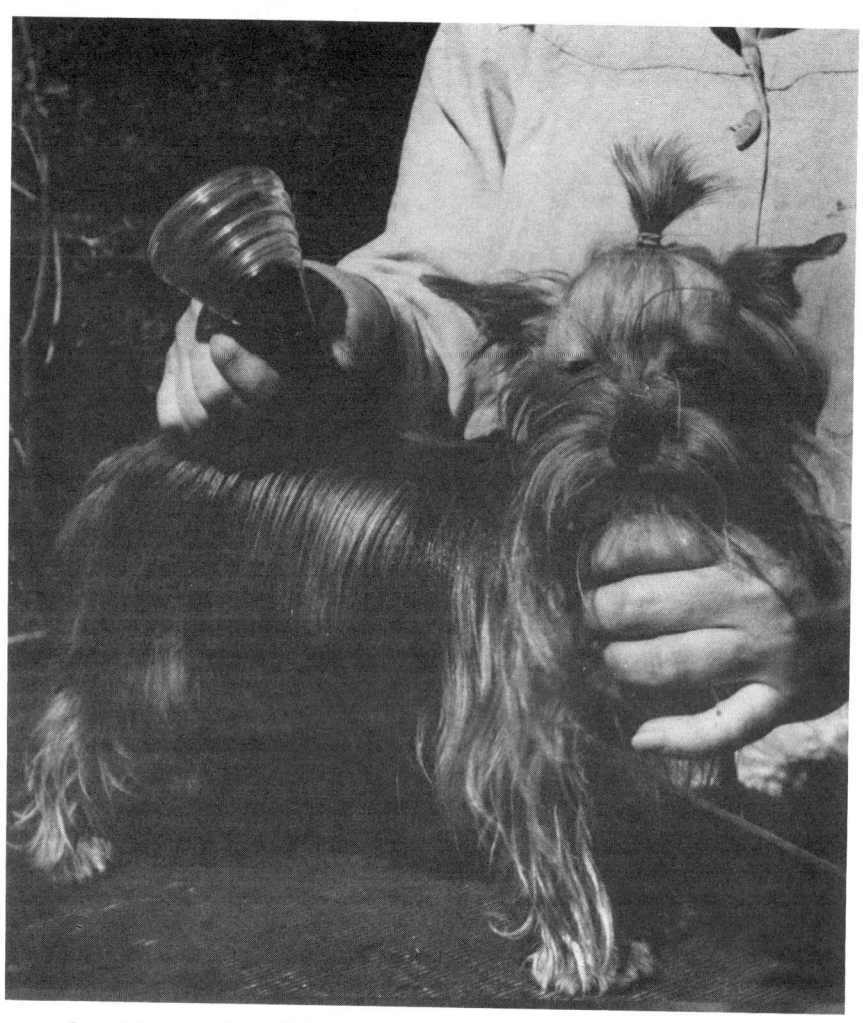

Special grooming oil keeps the Yorkie's long hair from matting.

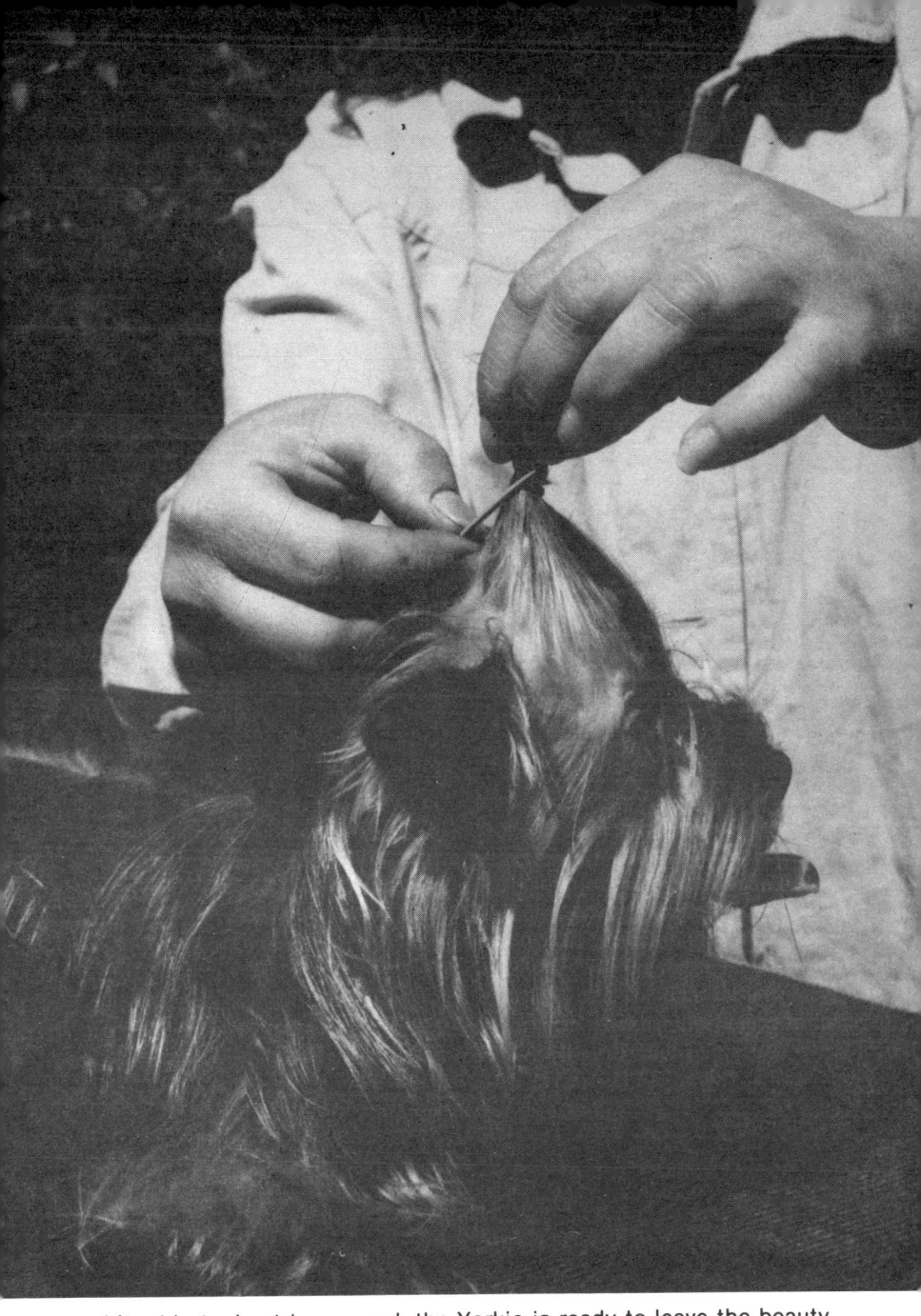

After his topknot is secured, the Yorkie is ready to leave the beauty parlor.

Constant conditioning is necessary to keep the coat of the Yorkshire Terrier ready for the show ring, but the beautiful end product is well worth the work.

56

7. Showing Your Yorkshire Terrier

One of the greatest thrills of owning a Yorkie is walking out of a show ring with a blue ribbon and a handful of silver trophies. Particularly with the Yorkie, a show "win" is a tribute to the owner's unceasing care of his pet as well as to the dog's natural attributes.

Basically the judge compares the dogs before him to the ideal dog as described in the standards of the breed, which you will find at the end of this chapter, and awards the prize to the dog that comes closest.

HOW TO ENTER

If your dog is purebred and registered with the American Kennel Club — or eligible for registration — you may enter him in the appropriate show class for which his age, sex and previous show record qualify him. You will find coming shows listed in the different dog magazines and in the "Yorkie Express," organ of the Yorkshire Terrier Club of America. Write to the secretary of the show, asking for the "Premium List." When you receive the entry form, fill it in carefully and send it back with the required entry fee. Then, before the show, you'll receive your Exhibitor's Pass which will admit you and your dog to the show.

Here are the five official show classes:

Puppy Class: Open to dogs at least 6 months and not more than 12 months of age. Limited to dogs whelped in the United States and Canada.

Novice Class: Open to dogs 6 months of age or older that have never won a first prize at a show — wins in puppy class excepted. Limited to dogs whelped in the United States or Canada.

Bred by Exhibitor Class: Open to all dogs except champions 6 months of age or over who are exhibited by the same person or kennel who was the recognized breeder on the records of the American Kennel Club.

American-Bred Class: Open to dogs that are not champions, 6 months of age or over, whelped in the United States after a mating which took place in the United States.

Open Class: Open to dogs 6 months of age or over, with no exceptions. In addition there are local classes, "special classes" and brace entries.

Separate classes are held for males and females and four places are awarded in each class. The male and female that win a first place in any class are qualified for the Winners Class which is also divided by sex.

Now, it gets complicated. Assume that you have a male Yorkie entered in the Puppy Class. He competes against other male puppies; meanwhile the female Yorkies in the Puppy Class are competing against each other. He wins first place in his Puppy Class, then competes against the winning males in the other classes. Here he gets the nod again and is now Winners Dog. Then, he earns a number of points towards his championship depending on the number of entries and other factors — just too complicated to go into here — but winning 15 points makes him a champion.

Next step is appearing in the ring against the Winners Bitch for the title Best of Winners. Then he may still have to face Yorkie champions who were entered in the Specials Class for the Best of Breed. Still tops, he goes against the winners in other toy dog classifications for Best of Group and finally meets the winners of other groups for the coveted Best in Show — the top dog of the show.

Before going into the hectic—and expensive—business of entering formal shows, you should get the opinions of some experts on your dog's potential and try him in some local Sanctioned Match Shows, which are informal shows held by dog clubs to give their members experience in the show ring and a chance to compare their dogs. The judging is usually done by qualified judges and the competition is keen even though the wins are not scored towards championships. The entry fee is usually around one dollar and no advance registration is necessary.

GETTING YOUR YORKIE READY FOR A SHOW

The Yorkie's coat is the most important factor in the show-ring judging so his pre-show grooming is vitally important. Bathe him the day before the show. First brush the tangles out of his hair, using a medium-length bristle brush. Do not use a nylon brush as it may break the hair. Using a good shampoo, gently lather downward with the pads of your fingers, and then rinse thoroughly. Wipe the moisture from the inside of his ears and pat him almost dry with a warm towel. Next stand him on a table and part his hair evenly from his nose to the end of his tail and brush down each side until dry. If you brush while he is damp, it will help prevent the hair from curling. Clip the hair from inside his ears and clean the ears and swab them with an antiseptic. The hair from the outside of his ears should be trimmed down about one inch from the tips, using the sharp, blunt end of the scissors. Make sure his nails are trimmed close and cut the hair in the pads of his feet. Trim the toe hair fringe, following the outline of his foot while the dog is standing. Check his teeth to make certain they are clean and wash his eyes with a very mild boric acid solution to give them a sparkling look.

Wrap the coat in papers.

The Yorkie, all groomed and shining, is in fine show form.

When you come to the show, remove the wrappers and brush the coat smooth. You may want to use a few drops of coat dressing. Brush the face fall forward for that typical, chipper Terrier expression. Comb the hair up and away from the eyes, parting it on each side from the corner of the eyes to the top inside of the ears and then straight across. Then gather up the head fall and tie it with a bright bow — and you're all set for the judging.

STANDARDS OF THE BREED

Once in the show ring, your Yorkie will be judged on these standards:

General Appearance: That of a long-haired toy terrier whose blue and tan coat is parted on the face and from the base of the skull to the end of the tail and hangs evenly and quite straight down each side of body. The body is neat, compact and well proportioned. The dog's high head carriage and confident manner should give the appearance of vigor and self-importance.

Head: Small and rather flat on top, the skull not too prominent or round, the muz-

The gait of the Yorkshire Terrier imparts the impression of elegance and confidence. High head carriage and ease of movement are breed trademarks.

zle not too long, with the bite neither undershot nor overshot and teeth sound. Either scissors bite or level bite is acceptable. The nose is black. Eyes are medium in size and not too prominent; dark in color and sparkling with a sharp, intelligent expression. Eye rims are dark. Ears are small, V-shaped, carried erect and set not too far apart.

Body: Well proportioned and very compact. The back is rather short, the back line level, with height at shoulder the same as at the rump.

Legs and Feet: Forelegs should be straight, elbows neither in nor out. Hind legs straight when viewed from behind, but stifles are moderately bent when viewed from the sides. Feet are round with black toenails. Dewclaws, if any, are generally removed from the hind legs. Dewclaws on the forelegs may be removed.

Tail: Docked to a medium length and carried slightly higher than the level of the back.

Coat: Quality, texture, and quantity of coat are of prime importance. Hair is glossy, fine and silky in texture. Coat on the body is moderately long and perfectly straight (not waxy). It may be trimmed to floor length to give ease of movement and a neater appearance, if desired. The fall on the head is long, tied with one bow in center of head or parted in the middle and tied with two bows. Hair on muzzle is very long. Hair should be trimmed short on tips of ears and may be trimmed on feet to give them a neat appearance.

Colors: Puppies are born black and tan and are normally darker in body color, showing an intermingling of black hair and tan until they are matured. Color of hair on body and richness of tan on head and legs are of prime importance in adult dogs, to which the following color requirements apply:

Blue: Is a dark steel-blue, not a silver blue and not mingled with fawn, bronzy or black hairs.

Tan: All tan hair is darker at the roots than in the middle, shading to still lighter tan at the tips. There should be no sooty or black hair intermingled with any of the tan.

Color on Body: The blue extends over the body from back of neck to roots of tail. Hair on tail is a darker blue, especially at end of tail.

Headfall: A rich golden tan, deeper in color at sides of head, at ear roots and on the muzzle with ears a deep rich tan. Tan color should not extend down on back of neck.

Chest and Legs: A bright, rich tan, not extending to the forelegs nor above the stifle on the hind legs.

Weight: Must not exceed seven pounds.

8. Breeding the Yorkshire Terrier

SIZE IS IMPORTANT

If you are planning to breed your female Yorkshire Terrier, size is an important factor. As the desirable weight today is about 4 pounds, you have a bit of a problem. A female 4 pounds or under usually requires a Caesarean delivery with the consequent expense and hazard. It is therefore best not to attempt to breed a small female. Instead, try to find a 5- to 7-pound female and breed her to a 2-pound stud with the same general bloodlines. Mixing two Yorkies with unrelated bloodlines may result in puppies that are larger than desirable.

Because of their small size Yorkies do not come in heat regularly as do most other breeds and you may have to wait almost a year for the proper time to mate your female.

Another factor in breeding Yorkies is that they are often rather poor mothers and may neglect their young. So if you are breeding, set in a supply of doll-sized milk bottles and nipples and get a formula from your vet in case you have the problem of suckling the puppies artificially.

PRE-NATAL CARE

Have your female examined by the vet before you mate her, especially to be certain that she is free of internal parasites. Usually this will require a microscopic examination of her stool and administration of the proper anti-worm treatment under the vet's supervision.

After the first week of pregnancy watch her diet, and increase her feeding schedule to three or four meals daily. To her usual menu, you should add milk, raw and cooked meat, cod-liver oil, wheat germ oil or brewer's yeast and some cereal. See that she gets boneless fish occasionally and plenty of calcium. Vitamin B complex and Vitamin D are important at this stage and should be provided by vitamin supplements. Let her lie in the sun as much as possible and permit her to exercise in moderation until the later period of gestation. Normally the gestation period is 63 days but many Yorkies seem to whelp a few days earlier.

Your rectal thermometer is a "must." Normal temperature is 100.6 to 101.5 and any variation should be checked with the vet. However, about a week before whelping it is normal for the temperature to drop to 98 or 99.

WHELPING

Shortly before her "time" the Yorkie will begin to pant and shiver, tear up papers and make a nest. You should prepare a place for her to deliver the puppies. A low, roomy box or carton is preferable. Cover the floor with heavy, corrugated cardboard, then over it place a strip of carpet and over that shredded newspapers. The dog needs a surface underfoot which she can grip with her claws.

Note the time when she first begins to strain. The uterine contractions will increase in frequency until the water bag appears—often in the form of bubbles—and shortly afterwards the first pup should appear. Just before delivery, the dog will be much occupied with her rear end, and you may hear her teeth grind as she severs the umbilical cord. If you want to help, you can tear the membrane from the face and head of the pup quickly so that it does not suffocate. Try to get a "yell" out of the pup. Dry it quickly with a soft towel and toss it from hand to hand until it gives a little yelp that indicates it's breathing properly.

When you are satisfied that the pup is all right, you can tear the cord about two inches from the pup, but do not tie it. Pull the cord of the afterbirth from the mother, not the pup, and try to remove the afterbirth. If you leave it, the mother will eat it and too much of it will have a laxative effect and kill her appetite for food.

As soon as you can, put the pup back with the mother and give her a chance to nuzzle and lick it. When the next becomes imminent (in about 20 minutes) remove the pup and put it in a box with warm blankets and a hot water bottle. Sometimes the delivery of later pups may be delayed for as much as an hour. If your dog is having a long whelping, feed her some glucose in milk, which is easily digestible. When the last pup has been born, the mother will want to relieve herself and will leave the box, giving you a chance to clean it up. Freshen the bed and put a warm hot water bottle or electric heating pad in one corner. The pups will thrive best if the room temperature is 70 to 80 degrees for a few days. After giving birth, the mother will need as many as five feedings a day for the next three days. Canned milk mixed with an equal amount of water and a little corn syrup added is a good feeding formula. Add a beaten egg to occasional feedings at this time, and keep her on a liquid diet for the next three days. After the third day—if her temperature is normal—begin putting her back on a normal diet. Check her temperature daily and call the vet if it reaches or goes over 103. A black or reddish discharge is normal for a few days, but a greenish discharge is a bad sign and you should call the vet. It is a good idea, too, for the vet to look over the mother and puppies, and you will want him to crop the pups' tails and remove the dewclaws.

WEANING THE PUPPIES

If the mother seems to be taking care of the puppy-feeding situation, leave her alone as interference from you may make her nervous. However, if she neglects the pups, or if there are some "shrimps" in the litter that are kept away from the nipples by larger and more active pups, get out the doll bottles and go to work. If you don't have a formula from your vet, a mixture of evaporated milk, corn syrup and some water, with an egg beaten in, served warm, should make a good puppy menu.

It may be necessary to trim the mother's coat short during the time she is with the pups as they will wreak havoc with her coat anyway.

When they are about three weeks of age you can begin to plate-feed the puppies, starting with a mushy mixture of baby cereals mixed with whole or evaporated milk. Make sure that they eat the food and do not use it as a wading pool. It's best to hold the plate a bit above the ground and feed two puppies at a time, keeping their paws out of the food. Follow each feeding with a cleaning-up, using a damp sponge. After they get the idea of eating from the plate, you can add broth or babies' soups to their menu. At about four weeks, they should be eating four meals a day and they should be stopped from suckling the mother at about five weeks. To dry up the mother, keep her away from the puppies for longer periods. After a few days of part-time nursing, she can stay away longer and longer and then completely. The little milk left in her body will be absorbed.

At six to eight weeks, the puppies are ready to start out to their future homes and begin the task of growing into beautiful adult Yorkies.